D0783159

Symphony No. 4
in G Major
for Soprano and Orchestra

Gustav Mahler

DOVER PUBLICATIONS, INC.
Mineola, New York

Copyright

Copyright © 2000, 2010 by Dover Publications, Inc.
All rights reserved.

Bibliographical Note

This Dover edition, first published in 2000 and reprinted in 2010, is a republication of the work originally published by Universal Edition, Vienna, n.d. [1906]. The poetic text, list of instruments, and score footnotes have been newly translated by Stanley Appelbaum. He graciously provided these materials as well as the glossary of German terms in the score. The prefatory note, page vi, was written specially for the Dover edition.

International Standard Book Number

ISBN-13: 978-0-486-41170-5
ISBN-10: 0-486-41170-2

Manufactured in the United States by Courier Corporation
41170204
www.doverpublications.com

CONTENTS

Symphony No. 4
in G Major
for Soprano and Orchestra

Composed 1892 and 1899–1901; revised 1910.
First performance: Munich, 25 November 1901

NOTE

Des Knaben Wunderhorn ("The Boy's Miraculous Horn") is a gathering of folksongs and folksong-style poems collected, retouched, or made up out of whole cloth by Achim von Arnin (1781–1831) and Clemens Brentano (1778–1842). The work was published in 1806 and 1808. Mahler's discovery of the collection, in 1887, began a lifelong exploration of its musical potential, providing the composer with all but one of his song texts over the next 14 years.

During his summer holiday of 1899, Mahler sketched two *Wunderhorn* settings; but after composing "Revelge" and with only ten days remaining, he found his Fourth Symphony suddenly beginning to take shape. In the early weeks of the new season he searched for a summer home where he could compose in peace, and eventually chose a site in Carinthia. There, in the following year, work on the Fourth Symphony was continued, then completed in 1901.

It was in this symphony that Mahler developed in its most sophisticated guise the idea of the programme. In this case, the poetic idea is the progress from experience (the first movement) to innocence (the *Wunderhorn* song finale, "Das himmlische Leben"— heavenly life). The progression is represented in a sequence of forms and textures that gradually diminishes in complexity until the utterly innocent vision of Paradise is attained in the concluding movement—the poetic and musical summit of an entire symphony.

With the admonition of its famous footnote (page 100)—"To be sung with childlike and serene expression; absolutely without parody!"—this is the work that closes Mahler's "Wunderhorn" period.

Freely adapted, in part, from Paul Banks' and Donald Mitchell's Mahler entry in *The New Grove Dictionary of Music and Musicians*, Vol. 11 (Macmillan Publishers Limited 1980)

TEXT AND TRANSLATION

DAS HIMMLISCHE LEBEN

Wir geniessen die himmlische Freuden,
d'rum thun wir das Irdische meiden.
Kein weltlich' Getümmel hört man nicht im Himmel!
Lebt Alles in sanftester Ruh'!
Wir führen ein englisches Leben!
Sind dennoch ganz lustig daneben!
Wir tanzen und springen, wir hüpfen und singen!
Sanct Peter im Himmel sieht zu!
Johannes das Lämmlein auslasset,
der Metzger Herodes drauf passet!
Wir führen ein geduldig's, unschuldig's, geduldig's
ein liebliches Lämmlein zu Tod!
Sanct Lucas den Ochsen thät schlachten
ohn' einig's Bedenken und Achten,
der Wein kost kein Heller im himmlischen Keller,
die Englein, die backen das Brot.
Gut' Kräuter von allerhand Arten,
die wachsen im himmlischen Garten!
Gut' Spargel, Fisolen und was wir nur wollen!
Ganze Schüsseln voll sind uns bereit!
Gut' Äpfel, gut' Birn' und gut' Trauben!
die Gärtner, die Alles erlauben!
Willst Rehbock, willst Hasen auf offener Strassen
sie laufen herbei! Sollt ein Festtag etwa kommen
alle Fische gleich mit Freuden angeschwommen!
Dort läuft schon Sanct Peter mit Netz und mit Köder
zum himmlischen Weiher hinein.
Sanct Martha die Köchin muss sein!
Kein Musik ist ja nicht auf Erden,
die uns'rer verglichen kann werden.
Elf tausend Jungfrauen zu tanzen sich trauen!
Sanct Ursula selbst dazu lacht!
Kein Musik ist ja nicht auf Erden,
die uns'rer verglichen kann werden.
Cäcilia mit ihren Verwandten
sind treffliche Hofmusikanten!
Die englischen Stimmen ermuntern die Sinnen,
dass Alles für Freuden erwacht.

HEAVENLY LIFE

We enjoy the heavenly delights,
therefore do we shun the earthly.
No worldly tumult is heard in heaven!
All live in balmiest peace!
We lead an angelic life!
But we are quite merry at the same time!
We dance and skip, we frisk and sing!
Saint Peter in heaven looks on!
John lets out the little lamb,
The butcher Herod lies in wait for it!
We lead a patient, innocent, patient,
darling little lamb to its death!
St. Luke slaughters the ox
without any hesitation or concern,
the wine costs not a penny in the heavenly cellar,
the angels bake the bread.
Good vegetables of every kind
grow in the heavenly garden!
Good asparagus, beans and whatever we may desire!
Whole tureens-full are prepared for us!
Good apples, good pears and good grapes!
the gardeners make room for everything!
If you want deer or hare, they come running to you
along the open road! Should a fast day perchance arrive,
all the fish swim by at once gladly!
There runs Saint Peter already with net and with bait
into the heavenly fishpond.
Saint Martha must be the cook!
There is truly no music on earth
with which ours can be compared.
Eleven thousand maidens venture to dance!
Saint Ursula herself laughs to see it!
There is truly no music on earth
with which ours can be compared.
Cecilia and her relatives
are excellent court musicians!
The angel voices enliven the senses,
So that everyone awakes for joy.

From *Des Knaben Wunderhorn*

GLOSSARY OF GERMAN TERMS
IN THE SCORE

(The words appear here exactly as they appear in the score.)

ab, off
abdämpfen, damp
aber, but
abnehmend, waning
abreissen, break off, flag
alle(s), all
allmählich, gradually
als, like, than
alten, old
am, at the
an, to
andern, others
Anfang(e), beginning
Anfangstempo, opening tempo
angebunden, played at the same time
Anmerkung, note
anmuthig, gracefully
anschwellend, crescendo
anzuschlagen, to be struck
As, A♭
auf, on, for
aufgehob., *aufgeh.*, *aufg.*, raised
aufgestellt, placed
aus, from
(sich) ausbreitend, broadening out
Ausdruck, expression
ausdrucksvoll, expressively
ausgeführt, played
auszuhalten, to sustain
B, B♭
Bässe, double basses
bedächtig, deliberate
befestigt, attached
beginnen, begin
behaglich, comfortable
bei, on
beide, both
beinahe, almost
besonders, especially
Betonungen, accentuation
bewegt, animated, agitated
bewegter, più mosso
Bewegung, motion, tempo
bezeichneten, marked
bis zum, until the
bitterlich, bitterly
bleiben, remain, *bleibt*, remains
Bogen, bow
brechen, arpeggiate
breit, broad, broadly, *breiter*, more broadly
Celli, cellos

Cis, C♯
Consonanten, consonant
Dämpfer, mute, mutes, muting
das, the
dasselbe, the same
dem, *den*, the
der, the, of the, who
Des, D♭
deutlich, clearly
die, the
diesen, this
Dirigenten, conductor
dirigiren, conduct, beat
doch, but
Doppelgriff, *Dopplgr.*, double stop
drängend, pressing, *drängender*, more pressing
dumpf, muffled, dull
durch, (obtained) through
durchaus, throughout
eben, just previously
ebenfalls, likewise
ebenso, just as
Echoton, echo tone
edlen, noble, exalted
eilen, hurry, *ohne zu eilen*, without hurrying
eilend, hurrying
eine, *einem*, a, one (player)
einer, *eines*, of a
einige, several
(sich) entfernend, becoming distant
Entfernung, distance
Empfindung, feeling, emotion
empfunden, (deeply) felt
entschieden, resolute
erste(n), first
ersterbend, dying away
Es, E♭
etwas, somewhat
Ferne, distance
feurige, fiery
Fidel, medieval fiddle
Figuren, figures
Fis, F♯
Flag., harmonics
fliessend, flowing
folgend, following, in keeping with
fort, continuing
fortlaufend(er), running, continuous
frei, freely
freihängend, suspended
frisch, vigorous, lively
früher, earlier
für, for

furchtbarer, formidable
ganzes, full
gänzlich, completely
gebrochen, arpeggiated
gebunden, legato
gedämpft, damped
gedehnt, drawn out
gehalten(en), held, held back, meno mosso
gehaltener, more restrained
geheimnisvoll(er), mysterious
gehen, go
gemächlich, comodo, easily, *gemächlicher*, più comodo
gemässigt(e), moderate
geringste, briefest
gerissen, cut off
Ges, G♭
gesangvoll, cantabile
gesättigten, saturated
geschlagen, struck
gestimmt, tuned
gestopft, *gest.*, stopped
gestrichen, bowed
gesungen, sung
getheilt, *geth.*, divisi
getragen, solemn
Gewalt, power
gewirbelt, rolled
gewöhnlich(e), ordinario, normally
Gis, G♯
gleichen, equal-sized
gleichmässiger, even
grell, shrill
Gr. Fl., flute
Griffbrett, fingerboard, sul tasto
grob, coarsely, rudely
grossem, *grosser*, great, large
grössere, larger
gut, quite
H, B
Halbe, (beat in) half-notes
Hälfte, half (of a string section)
Halt, pause
hart, hard
Hast, haste
Haupttempo, principal tempo
Hauptzeitmass, principal tempo
herausgestossen, thrust out
hervortretend, *hervortr.*, prominently
hier, here, *von hier an*, from here on
hinaufziehen, approaching from below
hinunterziehen, approaching from above
hoch, high

höchster, greatest
hohe, high
Höhe, elevation, in die Höhe, i. d. Höhe, up, in the air
höher, higher
Holzbläser, woodwinds
Holzschlägeln, wooden mallets
hörbar, audible
im, in, in the
immer, always
ja, absolutely
kaum, barely
keck, bold
keine, no
klagend, lamenting
Klang, sound
kleine, small
klingen, ring
klingt, sounds
Kopfstimme, head voice
Kraft, Kraftentfaltung, power
kräftig, robustly
kurz(er), short
Lage, position
lange, long
langhallenden, long-resounding
langsam, slow, langsamer, slower
(sich) lassen, allow
lebhaft, lively
leidenschaftlich, passionately
leise, softly
letzten, previous
lustig, merry, merrily
Marsch, march
mehr, more
mehrfach besetzt, several to a part
merklich, noticeably
mit, with
mittlere, medium, middle
möglich, possible
möglichst, as . . . as possible
munter, cheerfully
Musiker, musician
nach, (retune) to
nachgeben, broaden
nachhorchend, listening
nachlassen, relax
Nachschlag, Nachschl., turn (at end of trill)
nachzuahmen, to imitate
(sich) nähernd, drawing nearer
Naturlaut, sound of nature
natürlich, ordinario
nehmen, take, change to
nicht, not, don't
nimmt, take, change to
noch, still
Note, notes
Notfall, necessity, nur im Notfall zur, only if necessary for
nur, only
offen, open, unstopped
ohne, without
Oktav(e), octave

Orchester, orchestra
Piston, cornet, kleinem Piston, small cornet in E♭
plötzlich, suddenly, plözlichem, sudden
Pralltriller, mordents
Pulte, desks, stands
recht, quite, very
Rhythmus, rhythm
roh(er), rough, crude
Rücksicht, regard
ruhevoll, peaceful
ruhig, calm
Saite, string
sanft, soft
Satz, movement
Schalltrichter, Schalltr., bells (of wind instruments)
Schlägeln, mallets
schlagen, beat, conduct
schleppen, drag
Schluss, end
schmetternd, blaring, resounding
schnell, fast, schneller, faster
Schwammschlägeln, sponge mallets
schwer, heavy
Schwung, energy
schwungvoll, energetically
sehr, very
selben, same
singend, singing
so . . . als, as . . . as
sofort, immediately
Sordinen, mutes
Spieler, players, 2. Spieler, second group of 1st violins
spring. Bog., sautillé
stark, strongly, stärker, stronger, stärker besetzt, more players to a part
Steg, bridge
steigernd, intensifying
Steigerungen, increases
stetig, stets, steadily
Stimme, voice, group of 1st violins
Streicher, strings
streng, strictly
Strich, bowstroke, Strich für Strich, one bow per note, détaché
stürmen, rage, rush
summend, humming
Takt, beat, time
taktiren, tactiren, conduct, beat
Tellern, mit Tellern, clashed cymbals
Tempowechsel, change in tempo
Theilen, sections
tief(e), low, tiefer, lower
Ton, note, tone, sonority
Tönen, notes
Tonhöhe, register
Triangelschlägel, triangle beater
Triller, trill
Triolen, triplets
über, over, über das ganze Orchester hinaus, rising above the whole orchestra

Übergange, transition
übernimmt, takes, changes to
überraschend, surprisingly
übertönend, rising above, alles übertönend, louder than the rest of the orchestra
und, and
ungefähr, approximately
unmerklich, imperceptibly
Unterstützung, reinforcement, support
verändern, changing
verdoppelt, doubled
verhallend, becoming fainter
verklingend, dying away
Verlaufe, course
(sich) verlierend, dying away
Vermittlung, transition
verschwindend, disappearing
versehen, provided
versieht, plays
vibrirend, vibrating, with vibrato
viel, much, a lot of
Viertel, quarter-notes
Vokal, vowel
vollziehen, execute, vollzieht sich, to be executed
vom, by the
von, by
vorgetragen, played
vorhanden, (is) available
vorher, vorhin, before
Vorschläge, grace notes
vorwärts, pressing forward
wechseln, change
weich, soft, gently
Weise, tune, call
weiter, far, weitester, farthest
welche, which
wenig, little
wenn, if
werden, becoming
wie, as, as though
wieder, again
wild, unrestrained
womöglich, wo möglich, if possible
Worte, words
wuchtiger, more heavily, more vigorously
zart(e), gentle, gently, tenderly
Zeit, time
zögernd, hesitating
zu, to, in, at, zu 2, 3, 4, unisono
zuerst, at first
zufahrend, pressing, stringendo
zuletzt, just previously
zum, zur, to the
zurückhalten(d), meno mosso, zurückhaltender, more restrained
zurückkehren, return, zurückkehrend, returning
zwei, two
1., 2., 3., 4., 1st, 2nd, 3rd, 4th
2te, 3te, 4te, 2nd, 3rd, 4th
2(3,4) fach, in 2(3,4) parts

INSTRUMENTATION

4 Flutes [Flöte, Fl.]
  (Fl. 3,4 = Piccolo [Picc.] 1,2)
3 Oboes [Ob.]
  (Ob. 3 = English Horn [Englisch Horn, Englh.])
3 Clarinets (A,B♭,C) [Clarinette, Cl.]
  (Cl. 2 = E♭ Clarinet [Cl. in Es] ; Cl. 3 = Bass Clarinet
  (A,B♭) [Bassclarinet, Bcl. (A,B)])
3 Bassoons [Fagott, Fag.]
  (Bsn. 3 = Contrabassoon [Contrafagott, Ctrfag.])
4 Horns (F)
3 Trumpets (F,B♭) [Trompete,Trp. (F,B)]
Timpani [Pauke, Pk.]
Sleighbells [Schelle, Sch.]
Cymbals [Becken, Bck.]
Glockenspiel [Glspl.]
Triangle [Triangel, Trgl.]
Tam-tam
Bass Drum [Grosse Trommel, Gr. Tr.]
Harp [Harfe, Hfe.]
Violins I, II [Violine, Vl.]
Violas [Vla.]
Cellos [Violoncell, Vlc.]
Basses [Contrabass, Cb.]

Soprano [Singstimme, Singst.]

Symphony No. 4
in G Major

I.

+ Zeichen für einzelne gestopfte Töne.

+ Symbol for individual stopped tones.

172

NB. Klingt eine Octave tiefer.

II.

NB. Der 1. Sologeiger hat sich mit 2 Instrumenten zu versehen, von denen das eine um einen Ganzton höher, das andere normal gestimmt ist.

N.B. The 1st solo violin must be provided with two instruments, one tuned a whole-tone higher, the other tuned normally.

45

170
1.2. Fl.
1.2. Picc.
1.
Ob.
2.
1.
Cl.
in B.
2.
1. Fag.
1. Horn
in F.
1. Trp.
in F.
1. S.-Vl.
1.
Vl.
2.
Vla.
Vlc.
Cb.
lustig
zu 2
arco

322

333

343

III.

278

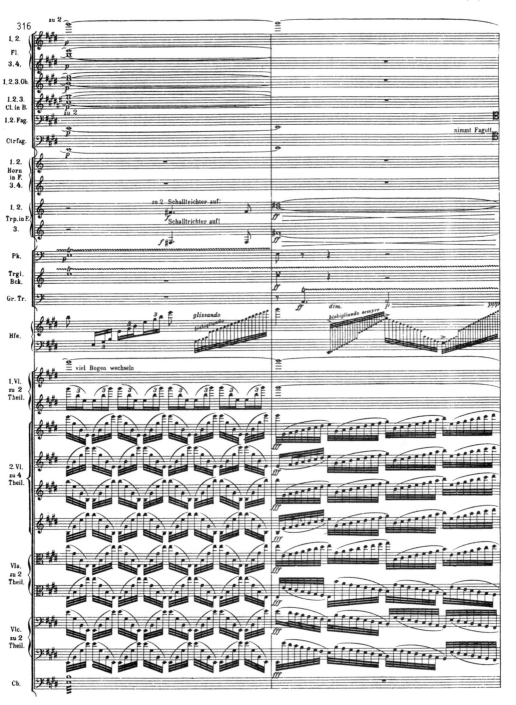

Anmerkung für den Dirigenten: Es ist von höchster Wichtigkeit,dass die Sängerin äusserst discret begleitet wird.

Note for the conductor: It is of the greatest importance that the singer be *extremely* discreetly accompanied.

IV.

NB. Singstimme mit kindlich heiterem Ausdruck; durchaus ohne Parodie!

N.B. To be sung with childlike and serene expression; absolutely without parody!

*) Hier muss dieses Tempo bewegter genommen werden, als an den correspondierenden Stellen im ersten Satze.

*) Here this tempo must be taken faster than at the corresponding passages in the first movement.

Ha - sen auf of - fe - ner Stra - ssen sie lau - fen her - bei! Sollt ein Fest-tag et - wa kommen al - le Fi - sche gleich mit

112

Ca - ci - lia mit ih - ren Ver - wan - - - - dten sind treff - li-che Hof - mu - si - kan - ten!

Die eng - lischen Stimmen er - mun - tern die Sin - nen, er - mun - tern die Sin - nen!

END OF EDITION

DOVER FULL-SIZE ORCHESTRAL SCORES

THE SIX BRANDENBURG CONCERTOS AND THE FOUR ORCHESTRAL SUITES IN FULL SCORE, Johann Sebastian Bach. Complete standard Bach-Gesellschaft editions in large, clear format. Study score. 273pp. 9 x 12. 23376-6

COMPLETE CONCERTI FOR SOLO KEYBOARD AND ORCHESTRA IN FULL SCORE, Johann Sebastian Bach. Bach's seven complete concerti for solo keyboard and orchestra in full score from the authoritative Bach-Gesellschaft edition. 206pp. 9 x 12. 24929-8

THE THREE VIOLIN CONCERTI IN FULL SCORE, Johann Sebastian Bach. Concerto in A Minor, BWV 1041; Concerto in E Major, BWV 1042; and Concerto for Two Violins in D Minor, BWV 1043. Bach-Gesellschaft edition. 64pp. 9⅜ x 12¼. 25124-1

GREAT ROMANTIC VIOLIN CONCERTI IN FULL SCORE, Ludwig van Beethoven, Felix Mendelssohn and Peter Ilyitch Tchaikovsky. The Beethoven Op. 61, Mendelssohn, Op. 64, and Tchaikovsky, Op. 35 concertos, reprinted from the Breitkopf & Härtel editions. 224pp. 9 x 12. 24989-1

SYMPHONIES NOS. 1, 2, 3, AND 4 IN FULL SCORE, Ludwig van Beethoven. Republication of H. Litolff edition. 272pp. 9 x 12. 26033-X

SYMPHONIES NOS. 5, 6 AND 7 IN FULL SCORE, Ludwig van Beethoven. Republication of the H. Litolff edition. 272pp. 9 x 12. 26034-8

SYMPHONIES NOS. 8 AND 9 IN FULL SCORE, Ludwig van Beethoven. Republicaticn of the H. Litolff edition. 256pp. 9 x 12. 26035-6

SIX GREAT OVERTURES IN FULL SCORE, Ludwig van Beethoven. Six staples of the orchestral repertoire from authoritative Breitkopf & Härtel edition. *Leonore Overtures*, Nos. 1–3; Overtures to *Coriolanus, Egmont, Fidelio.* 288pp. 9 x 12. 24789-9

COMPLETE PIANO CONCERTOS IN FULL SCORE, Ludwig van Beethoven. Complete scores of five great Beethoven piano concertos, with all cadenzas as he wrote them, reproduced from authoritative Breitkopf & Härtel edition. New table of contents. 384pp. 9⅜ x 12¼. 24563-2

THREE ORCHESTRAL WORKS IN FULL SCORE: Academic Festival Overture, Tragic Overture and Variations on a Theme by Joseph Haydn, Johannes Brahms. Reproduced from the authoritative Breitkopf & Härtel edition, three of Brahms's great orchestral favorites. Editor's commentary in German and English. 112pp. 9⅜ x 12¼. 24637-X

COMPLETE CONCERTI IN FULL SCORE, Johannes Brahms. Piano Concertos Nos. 1 and 2; Violin Concerto, Op. 77; Concerto for Violin and Cello, Op. 102. Definitive Breitkopf & Härtel edition. 352pp. 9⅜ x 12¼. 24170-X

COMPLETE SYMPHONIES, Johannes Brahms. Full orchestral scores. No. 1 in C Minor, Op. 68; No. 2 in D Major, Op. 73; No. 3 in F Major, Op. 90; and No. 4 in E Minor, Op. 98. Reproduced from definitive Vienna Gesellschaft der Musikfreunde edition. Study score. 344pp. 9 x 12. 23053-8

SYMPHONY NO. 5 IN B-FLAT MAJOR IN FULL SCORE, Anton Bruckner. Featuring strikingly original harmonies, an extended structure, and tonal range, this staple of the orchestral repertoire is a landmark of the Austro-Germanic symphonic tradition. 192pp. 9 x 12. (Available in U.S. only) 41691-7

THE PIANO CONCERTOS IN FULL SCORE, Frédéric Chopin. The authoritative Breitkopf & Härtel full-score edition in one volume of Piano Concertos No. 1 in E Minor and No. 2 in F Minor. 176pp. 9 x 12. 25835-1

COMPLETE CONCERTI GROSSI IN FULL SCORE, Arcangelo Corelli. All 12 concerti in the famous late-nineteenth-century edition prepared by violinist Joseph Joachim and musicologist Friedrich Chrysander. 240pp. 8⅜ x 11¼. 25606-5

THREE GREAT ORCHESTRAL WORKS IN FULL SCORE, Claude Debussy. Three favorites by influential modernist: *Prélude à l'Après-midi d'un Faune, Nocturnes,* and *La Mer.* Reprinted from early French editions. 279pp. 9 x 12. 24441-5

SYMPHONY NO. 8 IN G MAJOR, OP. 88, SYMPHONY NO. 9 IN E MINOR, OP. 95 ("NEW WORLD") IN FULL SCORE, Antonín Dvořák. Two celebrated symphonies by the great Czech composer, the Eighth and the immensely popular Ninth, "From the New World," in one volume. 272pp. 9 x 12. 24749-X

CELLO CONCERTO IN E MINOR, OP. 85, IN FULL SCORE, Edward Elgar. A tour de force for any cellist, this frequently performed work is widely regarded as an elegy for a lost world. Melodic and evocative, it exhibits a remarkable scope, ranging from tragic passion to buoyant optimism. Reproduced from an authoritative source. 112pp. 8⅜ x 11. (Not available in Europe or United Kingdom) 41896-0

SYMPHONY IN D MINOR IN FULL SCORE, César Franck. Superb, authoritative edition of Franck's only symphony, an often-performed and recorded masterwork of late French romantic style. 160pp. 9 x 12. 25373-2

HOLBERG SUITE AND OTHER ORCHESTRAL WORKS IN FULL SCORE, Edvard Grieg. Famed title work, five others: Two Elegiac Melodies, Op. 34; Old Norwegian Romances with Variations, Op. 51; Two Melodies, Op. 53; Lyric Pieces from Opp. 54 and 68. Authoritative C. F. Peters editions. 192pp. 9 x 12. 41692-5

COMPLETE CONCERTI GROSSI IN FULL SCORE, George Frideric Handel. Monumentai Opus 6 Concerti Grossi, Opus 3 and "Alexander's Feast" Concerti Grossi—19 in all—reproduced from most authoritative edition. 258pp. 9⅜ x 12¼. 24187-4

GREAT ORGAN CONCERTI, OPP. 4 & 7, IN FULL SCORE, George Frideric Handel. 12 organ concerti composed by great Baroque master are reproduced in full score from the *Deutsche Handelgesellschaft* edition. 138pp. 9⅜ x 12¼. 24462-8

WATER MUSIC AND MUSIC FOR THE ROYAL FIREWORKS IN FULL SCORE, George Frideric Handel. Full scores of two of the most popular Baroque orchestral works performed today—reprinted from definitive Deutsche Handelgesellschaft edition. Total of 96pp. 8⅜ x 11. 25070-9

SYMPHONIES 88–92 IN FULL SCORE: The Haydn Society Edition, Joseph Haydn. Full score of symphonies Nos. 88 through 92. Large, readable noteheads, ample margins for fingerings, etc., and extensive Editor's Commentary. 304pp. 9 x 12. (Available in U.S. only) 24445-8

THE PLANETS IN FULL SCORE, Gustav Holst. Spectacular symphonic suite, scored for large orchestral forces and a wordless chorus, embodies the astrological and mystical qualities of various planets. Only full-size score available. 192pp. 9⅜ x 12¼. (Not available in Europe or United Kingdom) 29277-0

THE PIANO CONCERTI IN FULL SCORE, Franz Liszt. Available in one volume: the Piano Concerto No. 1 in E-flat Major and the Piano Concerto No. 2 in A Major—among the most studied, recorded and performed of all works for piano and orchestra. 144pp. 9 x 12. 25221-3

PIANO CONCERTOS NOS. 1 AND 2 IN FULL SCORE, Edward MacDowell. Glittering keyboard displays, surging emotional appeal, and a grand heroic manner characterize these popular late–nineteenth-century works. Introduction by Dr. Brian Mann. Instrumentation. 224pp. 9 x 12. 42666-1

DAS LIED VON DER ERDE IN FULL SCORE, Gustav Mahler. Mahler's masterpiece, a fusion of song and symphony, reprinted from the original 1912 Universal Edition. English translations of song texts. 160pp. 9 x 12. 25657-X

SYMPHONIES NOS. 1 AND 2 IN FULL SCORE, Gustav Mahler. Unabridged, authoritative Austrian editions of Symphony No. 1 in D Major ("Titan") and Symphony No. 2 in C Minor ("Resurrection"). 384pp. 8⅜ x 11. 25473-9

SYMPHONIES NOS. 3 AND 4 IN FULL SCORE, Gustav Mahler. Two brilliantly contrasting masterworks—one scored for a massive ensemble, the other for small orchestra and soloist—reprinted from authoritative Viennese editions. 368pp. 9⅜ x 12¼. 26166-2

TONE POEMS, SERIES II: TILL EULENSPIEGELS LUSTIGE STRE-ICHE, ALSO SPRACH ZARATHUSTRA, and EIN HELDENLEBEN, Richard Strauss. Three important orchestral works, including very popular *Till Eulenspiegel's Merry Pranks,* reproduced in full score from original editions. Study score. 315pp. 9⅜ x 12¼. (Not available in Europe or United Kingdom)   23755-9

THE FIREBIRD IN FULL SCORE (Original 1910 Version), Igor Stravinsky. Handsome, inexpensive edition of modern masterpiece, renowned for brilliant orchestration and glowing color. Authoritative Russian edition. 176pp. 9⅜ x 12¼. (Available in U.S. only)   25535-2

FIREWORKS AND SONG OF THE NIGHTINGALE IN FULL SCORE, Igor Stravinsky. *Fireworks* is a brilliant early score written in 1908; *Song of the Nightingale* is a symphonic poem for orchestra. 128pp. 9 x 12 . (Available in U.S. only)   41392-6

PETRUSHKA IN FULL SCORE: Original Version, Igor Stravinsky. The definitive full-score edition of Stravinsky's masterful score for the great Ballets Russes 1911 production of *Petrushka.* 160pp. 9⅜ x 12¼. (Available in U.S. only)   25680-4

THE RITE OF SPRING IN FULL SCORE, Igor Stravinsky. A reprint of the original full-score edition of the most famous musical work of the 20th century, created as a ballet score for Diaghilev's Ballets Russes. 176pp. 9⅜ x 12¼. (Available in U.S. only)   25857-2

FOURTH, FIFTH AND SIXTH SYMPHONIES IN FULL SCORE, Peter Ilyitch Tchaikovsky. Complete orchestral scores of Symphony No. 4 in F minor, Op. 36; Symphony No. 5 in E minor, Op. 64; Symphony No. 6 in B minor, "Pathetique," Op. 74. Study score. Breitkopf & Härtel editions. 480pp. 9⅜ x 12¼.   23861-X

NUTCRACKER SUITE IN FULL SCORE, Peter Ilyitch Tchaikovsky. Among the most popular ballet pieces—a complete, inexpensive, high-quality score to study and enjoy. 128pp. 9 x 12.   25379-1

ROMEO AND JULIET OVERTURE AND CAPRICCIO ITALIEN IN FULL SCORE, Peter Ilyitch Tchaikovsky. Two of Russian master's most popular compositions in high quality, inexpensive reproduction. From authoritative Russian edition. 208pp. 8⅜ x 11¼.   25217-5

GREAT OVERTURES IN FULL SCORE, Carl Maria von Weber. Overtures to *Oberon, Der Freischutz, Euryanthe* and *Preciosa* reprinted from authoritative Breitkopf & Härtel editions. 112pp. 9 x 12.   25225-6

Paperbound unless otherwise indicated. Available at your book dealer, online at **www.doverpublications.com** or by writing to Dept. 23, Dover Publications, Inc., 31 East 2nd Street, Mineola, NY 11501. For current price information or for free catalogs (please indicate field of interest), write to Dover Publications or log on to **www.doverpublications.com** and see every Dover book in print. Dover publishes more than 500 books each year on science, elementary and advanced mathematics, biology, music, art, literary history, social sciences, and other areas.

Manufactured in the U.S.A.